PRAISE MY PET!

ADULT COLORING BOOK

WWW.PRAISEMYPET.COM

Color Alvin!

Color
Stella Rene'!

Hershey

Color Hershey!

6

Color
Kiwi and Pebbles Miranda!

Color Bow!

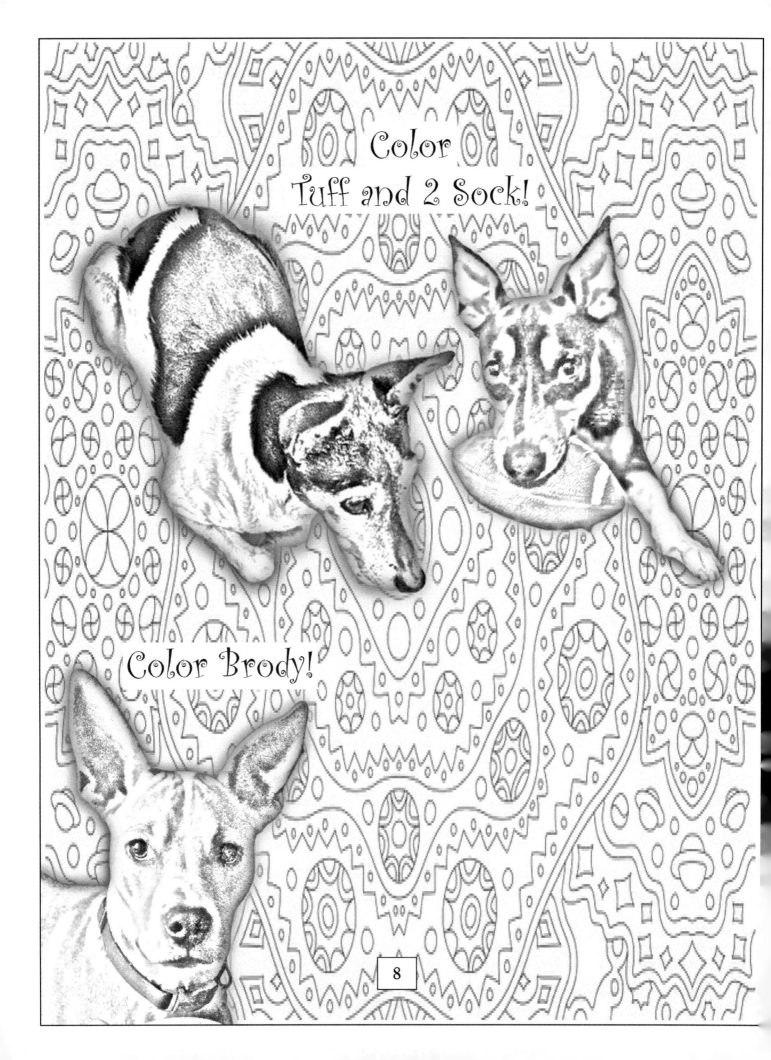

Color
Tuff and 2 Sock!

Color Brody!

Color
Gabby and Laken!

Color Tenga!

Color
Meow and September!

Color
Diesel and Sussudio!

Color Gemma!

Color Maddie!

11

Color

Miks, Minmay, Morena, Mouse and Simba!

12

Color Cinderella!

Color Ellie!

13

Color Jake!

15

Color
Pooper and Princess!

Color Millie!

17

Color Sophie!

19

Color Patches!

Color
Darrell and Ellie Mae!

20

Color Axel!

Color Spice!

22

Color Lilly!

23

Color Paris!

27

Color
Bella and Benny!

Color Sunnie!

28

Color
Grace and Hope!

Color Tiny!

31

Color
Bob, Nubs,
Willy and Tipper!

32

Color Zoey!

Color Belle!

35

Color
Bella and Sophie!

Color Oscar!

Color
Jack and Karlie!

37

Color Max!

38

Color
Mabel and Trudie!

Color Maggie Sue!

Color
Merlin and Sullivan!

41

Color Cowlie!

Color Tigger!

42

Color Piper!

Color
Bullet and Mosi!

43

Color Booboo!

Color
Rocket Dog!

44

45

Color Blue!

Color Molly!

46

Color Katie!

Color Gus!

47

Color Lily Joy!

Color Sadie Tip!

48

Color Lola!

Color Grizzabella!

49

Color
Pepper, Shorty and Joye!

50

Color Ernie!

Color
Heartley and Sasha!

51

Color
Peeping Tom!

Color
Rosco and Peach!

52

Color Stella!

Color Zach!

53

Color
BeBe and Lucy!

54

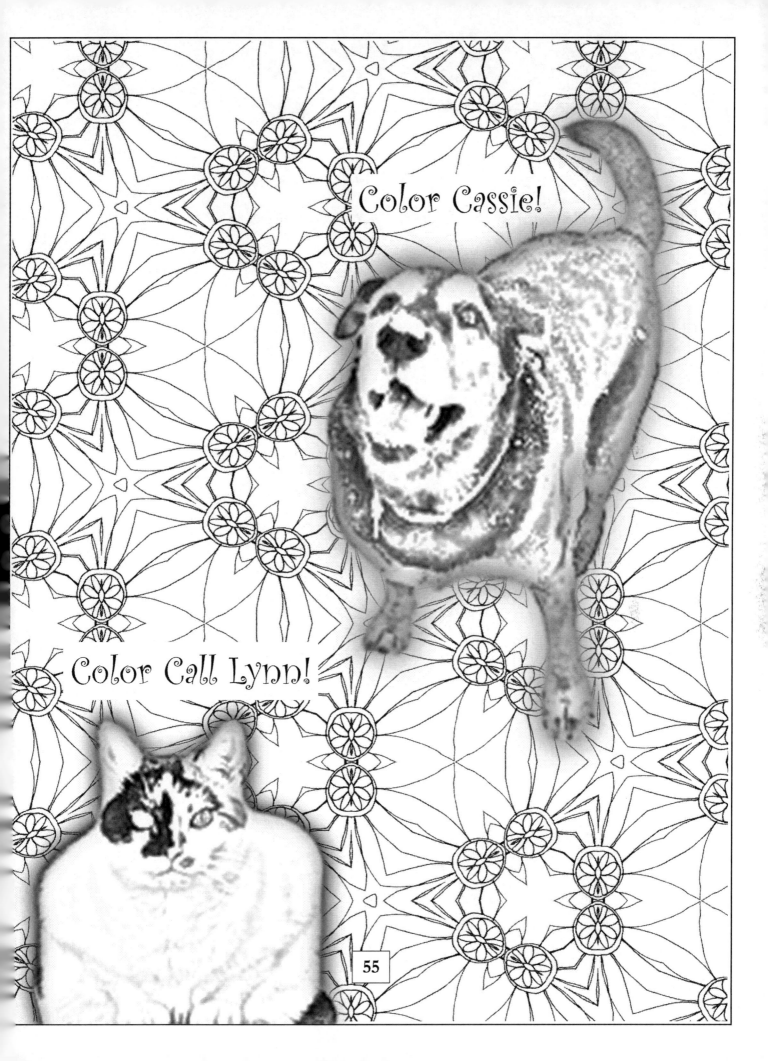

Color Cassie!

Color Call Lynn!

55

Color
Deedee and Ziggy!

56

Color Wednesday!

Color Lola!

Color Panda Bear!

Color Molly!

59

Color
Patches and Roscoe!

Color
Harley Quinn!

Color Choppers!

61

Color Lucy! Color Sally!

Color Spykey!

Color Kreesie Bear!

Color Cleo!

Color Maui!

Color Chance!

65

Color Max!

Color Charley!

67

Color
Yogi, Angel and Babygirl!

68

Color Charlie!

Color Little Bit!

69

Color CuJoe!

Color Daisy!

70

Color
Miss Pickles and Cheese!

71

Color Bentley!

Color
Miss Libby!

72

Color Zing!

Color Charolette!

73

Color
Lacey and Luke!

Color Cheyenne!

74

Color
Miss Onion and Otto!

76

Color
Mugsy and Malone!

Color Link!

77

Color Kona!

78

Color Mocha!

Color Lulu!

Color
Rudy and LuLu!

Color Jewel!

82

Color Kunani!

Color Rebel!

83

Color Joey!

Color Buddy!

84

...Color
Boss and Buffy!

Color Torty!

85

Color Archer!

Color Sampson!

Color
Kylee Mae and Annie Rose!

Color
Waldo E. Pupperbutt!

87

Color
Gabrielle Sapphire
and Prancer!

Color Spec!

89

Color Zoey Daisy!

Color Bernie!

90

Color Bandit!

Color Mooie and Falcor!

91

Color Bella!

Color
Daisy and Molly!

92

Color Elvis!

Color Elsa!

Color Mr. Smooth!

95

Color Gibbs!

Color Harley!

Color
Nala and Bella!

Color
Oreo and Dixie!

98

Color
Stella, Luna and Gio!

Color Shadow!

99

Color
Misti and Bayja!

Color
Bella and Rocky!

100

Color
CeCe, Reeko and Nemo!

101

Color
Lil Bit and Feisty!

Color
Gunner and Hershel!

102

We hope you enjoyed our coloring book! If you'd like to see YOUR pet in one of our upcoming coloring books, visit www.praisemypet.com/pages/send-us-your-pet-photos

Happy coloring!

Made in the USA
Columbia, SC
20 February 2021